MW00345650

# Happy Thoughts
## *To Keep and Give Away*

By
**Jack C. Kelley**
•

Lutz (Tampa), Florida 33549

*To Shirley*
*Always Keep a smile*
*in your heart &*
*on your face*
*:) Jack*

Copyright © 1996 Happy Thoughts To Keep and Give Away,
By Jack C. Kelley

All rights reserved. Printed in the United States of America.
For information:
Cameron Graphics Inc.
14199 SW Millikan Way
Beaverton, OR 97005
Ph# (503) 643-3331
ISBN 0-9658046-0-7

Grateful Acknowledgments for
Editorial Assistance:
*Sherri Ladislas*
*Elizabeth Macy*
*Anne Kelley*
*Doris Wheeler*

## Dedication

This book is dedicated to **Jay Wheeler** for his untiring editorial work and advice.

# FOREWORD

## Which of These Fit Your Face?

Happy 😊  Glad 😐  Angry ☹

I like happy people, do you?  Which of these faces do you wear?  Only you can decide.  Are you usually HAPPY, GLAD, or ANGRY?  Think about this.  You don t have to dress up to love God.  You can wear different socks or even no socks.  You see, God looks at the heart and if you have smiles in your heart, the smiles will splash out on your face.  God can't change your face, but he can change your heart.  If you let him change your heart, your face changes, too!

Most of us like to be around people who are happy and wear smiles.  Too often it is difficult to find happy people because many have let the world and its SADNESS TURN THEIR SMILES INTO FROWNS.  Kousin Zeke sez, "A radical heart transplant and even a face-lift shore could improve some of the sourpusses."

Let me make a suggestion, the next time you are in a griping and miserable mood, take a peek in a mirror and see what your family and friends have to endure.  Kousin Zeke is right.  A face-lift would be a smart and quick witted decision.  PLEASE, PLEASE DON'T WAIT UNTIL TOMORROW TO BEGIN SMILING.  Start smiling today, right now, this very moment.  BE A HAPPY FACE AND EACH DAY UNWRAP GIFTS OF SMILES AND SHARE YOUR SMILE GIFTS WITH OTHERS.

*Jack C. Kelley*
*alias "Kousin Zeke"*

### About The Author

*Jack C. Kelley is a free lance writer, author, and pastor. He is a licensed pilot and served in the U.S. Navy.*

*The "Happy Thoughts" in this collection have been published in major newspapers and periodicals. Through them Jack hopes to make a difference in this world by getting people to return to the basics of plain ol' common sense decency. This, in turn, will make for a happier, safer and better world. These "Happy Thoughts" are not preachy but helpful, cheerful, and spiced with humor. Each is a recipe for a HAPPY, HAPPY, DAY.*

QUOTABLE QUOTE

Kousin Zeke sez:
"What we all need is a little
dab of common sense."

"

# ABOUT THIS PUBLICATION

## How To Share Happiness With This Collection

The pages of this publication have been PERFORATED so they can be TORN OUT and SHARED with family and friends. Just remove the page and pass it along. Better yet, make copies so you can share a Happy Thought with lots of folks. After each message, there is a blank area for you to write a personalized note to the person who will receive the article. It's a great one stamp investment!

# CONTENTS

**TITLE**                                                                                 **PAGE**

# CONTENTS

# If You're Feeling Blue

What advice would you give someone who is depressed, discouraged and a candidate for a nervous breakdown? Since most of the world is infected with selfishness, it would be difficult for most of us to give any kind of sensible, helpful advice.

If he knew he was on the verge of a nervous breakdown, renowned psychiatrist Dr. Carl Menninger said, "I'd go out, find somebody in need, and help them."

Many believe money, fame and status will provide happiness and peace of mind. Nothing is further from the truth.

Are you discouraged or hurting? Do you know someone who is depressed and at their wit's end? Go today, or even at this moment, and become a friend in need and deed. You will be genuinely blessed, and so will those you befriend.

# Giving

What do you expect from life?  Believe it or not, what you give decides what you receive.  Someone wrote:

> I bargained with life for a penny,
> And life would pay me no more.
> And I had to beg in the evening,
> When I counted my scanty store.
> For life is a just employer,
> He gives you what you ask.
> But once you have set the wages,
> Why, you must bear the task.
> I worked for a menial hire,
> Only to learn dismayed,
> That any wage I had asked of life,
> Life gladly would have paid.

You may think or say, "I'm limited, I cannot give."  No one is limited in the caring love they can share with others.  Life pays well, when we give.  It is when we choose not to give that we lose.

*Be a winner and give generously.*

# Counting Blessings Can Ease Frustration

Have you ever been caught in a traffic jam on an interstate, surrounded by huge semi rigs, cars and lanes of traffic? If you haven't, you will be. All you can do is stare and wait, and wait, and wait.

One man described a traffic jam this way: "Sandwiched between two monsters, all I can do is stare at the back doors of the truck ahead and read how much each carrier pays in yearly taxes. I feel my patience running low and my adrenaline high." There is a way out. We can either fight it, fuss at it, or take a few moments to consider our plight. Ask ourselves, "What can I do about it, except wait?"

Calm down ... look at the sky or the trees. Change your thought agenda. Then begin to count your many, many blessings. Share a smile or a kind comment with another frustrated driver. Try it the next time you are in a stressful dilemma. Most of your frustrations will fade away, and even an inward smile can spill out.

# What's Your Definition of Happiness?

You may not know it, but every Tom, Dick, Harry and Jane is attempting to hard-sell you their definition of happiness, like it or not.  You are usually brainwashed in this manner:

- *You've Come A Long Way Baby*
- *Diet Secrets That Work*
- *Win Millions With Lotto*
- *The Ultimate Pleasure*
- *50% Off*
- *This Bud's For You*
- *Xmas in July*

The choicest definition I've heard is, "Happiness is not the absence of conflict but the ability to cope with it."  Until we learn how to cope with life's struggles, living can become "tough sledding" and much "easier said than done".  But it is very possible to be a content and happy person. It is up to each of us within ourselves.  If we lack contentment, we need to examine our own thinking and attitudes.

*Prevention Magazine* gave five rules for happiness.  I've adapted them somewhat:

1. Always look on the brighter side of life.
2. Accept cheerfully the place in life that is yours and live it to the fullest.
3. Put your soul and spirit into your work and give it your best.
4. Get into the habit of doing kindnesses and courtesies for others.
5. Adopt and maintain a simple childlike attitude of confidence and trust in God and Jesus.

*Living by these rules can only comfort and help*
*if we even halfway attempt to live and abide by them.*
LET'S TRY!!!

# Anxiety

A lady overwhelmed by anxiety said, "I feel like I m running from a dark cloud." Someone else said, "I'm boxed in and can't get out." Have you ever been there? Possibly you are there now. Anxiety may not kill you, but you might wish you were dead. A national clinic reported that anxiety is the number one emotional problem in America. One in ten men and one in five women will have a problem with anxiety. Left uncontrolled it can ruin lives, families, careers, marriages and friendships.

Anxiety is characterized by useless worry, fear, anger, hate, scary thoughts, mood swings, panic attacks, depression, feeling alone, hopelessness, guilty feelings, and an inability to eat or sleep. Often a chance incident can create a situation where we cannot cope or even make trivial decisions. How is it possible to win out, feel better, prevent crises from becoming anxieties? Here are some suggestions:

1. Realize we will look and feel better when we conquer our anxieties.
2. Think about the good side of life and forget the bad.
3. Stop dwelling on the past. It's finished — done and gone.
4. Try God's way. He understands our needs. That's the reason He sent Jesus, to give us peace.
5. Never forget, drugs and alcohol are not a solution.
6. Be thankful and decide you want to be someone others want to be with and around.

*Share your blessings with someone who is hurting.*
*Now That's Some Good Thinking!!!*

# Clean Machine Needed

A man traveling on a highway saw a "Dirt For Sale" sign.  He said, "They ought to hang that over every rack of paperback books, magazines and adult XXX stores all across America.  Not since Manhattan Island was sold for $24 has there been so much dirt available for so little money as now."

Doesn't that bother you?  It should!  Think of all the children, teens, grandchildren and the dirt they have to flow through.  Let's not forget the dirt and trash we all are bombarded with in movies and on television.

Do you have "Dirt" in your life, language, family or business?  If so, will it take a shovel or a bulldozer to scrape it up?

Let's go into the bulldozer business, not tomorrow, but TODAY.  Now would be the best time to begin.

# The Spirit of Santa Claus

"First I believed in Santa Claus; next I didn't believe. Then I discovered I was Santa Claus," the man said. Do you still believe in Santa Claus? I do! YEP, I believe in the spirit of generosity, giving and concern for others.

Many get hung up on self and receiving, so much so, that they become despicable, grasping and unhappy Scrooges. It is difficult for a Scrooge to discover the real you and the meaning of Christmas.

God's gift, broadcast by an angel, "The most wonderful news ever announced, it is to everyone, the Savior has been born" to give eternal life, peace and joy.

Do you desire a touch of joy and happiness to overflow and spill out on others? If so, become addicted to daily giving and sharing loving concern for the lonely and hurting.

I promise if you try it, you'll like it. Your loving concern will stick a smile on your face, and place smiles in the hearts of others. If you doubt it, check out the new Scrooge.

# Gentle Smile, Kind Thoughts

Have you realized that the marks of a mean, nasty temper, resentment and evil thoughts can be seen in a wrinkled brow, a drooped mouth and scornful eyes?

Abraham Lincoln objected to a certain appointment because he did not like the candidate's face. Someone responded, "But Mr. Lincoln, a man cannot help how he looks." Lincoln replied, "He can't help how he looks when he comes into the world, but he can help how he looks after 40 years."

A pleasant smile can replace a frowning countenance and remove a drooping mouth. Looking for the best in others will dispose of spiteful eyes. This facial make-over will do more for your countenance than a case of expensive soap or a $35 facial.

Think it over the next time you look in the mirror. Can you improve the person looking back? For some, even their dog will appreciate the improvement!

# Attitude and Ability Count More Than One's Age

I'm just too old. I'm over 40, 50, 60 or 70. What can I accomplish? I'm over the hill and I have few talents, if any. What's the use? I'm destined to be a nobody. You can't kid me; you see, I know me.

Let me share with you some people who would not subscribe to the above opinions and attitude for one second.

- *George Bernard Shaw wrote a play at 94.*
- *Grandma Moses was still painting at 100.*
- *Arthur Rubinstein gave a recital at Carnegie Hall at 89.*
- *Winston Churchill wrote "The History Of The English-Speaking People" at 82.*

What response would you receive from one of these persons if you said, "I'm too old to do anything?" What about you and me? As long as we have the will, a little bit of faith, and the get up and go, there will always be opportunities to produce and serve.

As long as there is one needy person in the world, we have something to do. Age is not the deciding factor.

*Never give up. Just do what falls across your path!*

# Moving an Inch Means a Lot in the Long Run

Did you ever say, "I'm not going to budge an inch. Nobody's going to walk over me or tell me what to do?"

I read a story about two rugged mountain goats who met on a narrow path joining two mountain ridges - on one side, a chasm 1,000 feet deep, on the other, a steep cliff rising straight up. So narrow was the trail that there was no room to turn around, and the goats could not back up without falling. What would they do? Instead of fighting for the right to pass, one of the goats knelt down and made himself flat. The other goat then walked over him, and they both proceeded safely.

Our ego usually rears its head and we say, "No way, and I mean no way, and that is it." But there comes a time when it's best to let others have their way, or even let them walk all over us. For most, this is unthinkable. However, it is not a sign of weakness, but one of strength and humility.

One fact is assured, if you are as smart as the goats, it will make traveling the road of life easier and more enjoyable.

# Television:  Friend or Foe?

TV - friend or foe, good or bad?  How do you decide?  Verna MacBeth wrote, "The TV can be a friend.  For those who are sick, it's a godsend.  For friends who grieve, it's company.  For news and weather, you'll agree, it keeps us posted day or night.  Some music - pure delight.  Some comedies can makes us laugh and cut our doctor bills in half.  Some children's programs make learning fun.  TV belongs in nursing homes, schools and homes.  The TV set, controlled, can bring us close to God: an awesome thing!"

But the downside is the over-abundance of violence, sex, profanity, alcohol and just plain old filth.  You name it and you've seen it on TV.  Television, left uncontrolled, can bring havoc to the family and even a nation.  TV controlled by common sense decency and Godly wisdom can help us to know when to turn the knob on, off, or to another channel.  The TV knob can be used to shut out the trash and invite the best into our minds and homes.

A 4th grade teacher told a pupil, "Be selective about the kinds of books you read."  She went on to say, "Our minds are like a prison cell in which we will spend the rest of our lives, so we must be careful how we furnish it."  This truth applies to your eyes, so be cautious what your eyes see.  The teacher was saying that since our minds and bodies are the home of Christ, we should be careful what we invite in.  A daily dose of dirt can affect our attitude and behavior.  If you question this, read the papers or watch TV.  The choice is yours and mine.  Decide to make TV a friend and not a foe.

*Do it now,*
*tomorrow is already too late*!!

# Hugging is Healthy

I read that hugging is healthy. Did you ever hear that? It would be difficult to prove, since a hug cannot be placed in a test tube. Someone wrote, "A sincere hug cures stress and depression. It is nothing less than a miracle drug." Hugging is all natural; it is organic, naturally sweet, no pesticides, no preservatives, no artificial ingredients and 100% wholesome.

Hugging is practically perfect; there are no movable parts, no batteries to wear out, no periodic check-ups, low-energy consumption, high-energy yield, inflation-proof, non-fattening, no monthly payments, no insurance requirements, theft-proof, non-taxable, non-polluting and, of course, fully returnable.

Do you know someone, a family member or friend, who needs a little TLH (Tender Loving Hug)? A loving, sincere hug may be what the doctor ordered for you or someone else. One fact is certain, it s better than taking pills!

# Be That Difference

In high school, he was not considered the student most likely to succeed. On a scale of one to ten, his self-esteem would be close to one. On the social scale, he would be voted very shy. He never asked a girl for a date and he failed every subject in high school. You could conclude that he was a born loser and would never succeed at anything. Even with a tutor he would probably be a flop.

But guess what? He became the world's most famous cartoonist and author, illustrating and writing for newspapers, books, magazines and television world-wide. He inspired and challenged millions to a happier and better way of life by his messages in cartoons. His name is Charles Schulz, creator of the *Peanuts* comic strip. Who could ever forget Charlie Brown, Linus, Lucy and Snoopy?

Charles Schulz evidently didn't moan and groan about what he couldn't do or have. Instead he used his God-given talent to the best of his ability. Believe in yourself and never say, "I can't." You may never be famous, but be the best with your talents and you can make a big difference in this world. God only knows, the world needs a big difference, for the good, that is.

*Be That Difference*!!!

# They Are Not Lost

In the comic strip *Dennis The Menace*, cartoonist Hank Ketcham teaches his readers a fact of life necessary for peace of mind. The first scene shows Dennis sitting on a park bench with his mother and a friend, Mrs. Lewis. Dennis says, "How come we're sitting here?" His mother says, "Dennis - Please!" Her friend was upset and said, "I just lost my dad." Dennis replied, "Didn't you just say you lost your dad?" Mrs. Lewis says, "Yes, I did say that but..." "Well, let's go. I'll help ya look!" Dennis responded. Mrs. Lewis said, "But I didn't lose him in the park."
"Then where did you lose him?" asked Dennis.
"In the hospital," Mrs. Lewis replied sadly.

Dennis' mother called him over and began to whisper in his ear. Then Dennis said, "Ooohh! Well, why didn't you say so?" Dennis then said to Mrs. Lewis, "You didn't lose your dad, God took him! And when God takes somebody they're not lost! They're okay 'cuz they're with God! Do you understand Mrs. Lewis?" She replied, "I do now, Dennis."

That is a priceless lesson to learn and know. Dennis hit the nail on the head. We become so caught up with the fashion of this world and its things and junk that we won't be prepared for God's call when our number pops up. It will. Two facts of life we cannot avoid: Death and Taxes. There is a road map and compass for life's direction — God's Word. Read, study and obey it. Otherwise you may have to call on Dennis to explain God's plan to you.

Kousin Zeke sez, "A friend told me he shore had plenty of time and he was going to eat, drink and make merry and not worry 'bout his Christian faith until the clock hit 11:59. I tell's him, You shore gonna miss lots of fun, and what are you gonna do when your number pops up BEFORE 11:59?"

# Two Neglected Words

Do you know the two most neglected words in the dictionary? Most people have no idea and could care less. Once a year our nation observes a special day of thanks, but even then the two words are seldom used. Lest you have forgotten, the special day is Thanksgiving and the two neglected words are THANK YOU. Someone asked a man, "Is thank you written as one word or two words?" He replied, "I don't know I never use the words."

Even Jesus, who reminded us to always be thankful, had to deal with thankless people who had forgotten how to say thank you. He healed ten lepers and only one returned to thank him. He asked, "Where are the other nine, did only one return to give glory to God?" I would have asked, "Where in the cotton-pickin' world are the other thankless ones?"

An atheist made fun of a father who always gave thanks before meals. The father said, "You remind me of my hogs when I feed them, they dive right in and never once look up." We, too, should be cautious lest we substitute GIMME for THANK YOU. How? By being thankful for God's love and forgiveness and never failing to pass on a thank you to friends, enemies, or whoever.

One fact is certain. When we share a thank you, we will be blessed and so will those we thank.

**MAKE EVERY DAY A THANKSGIVING DAY.**
*Try it, you'll like it!!!*

# Just Say No

A radio station blared out, "GET HIGH - GET STUPID - GET AIDS". Billboards on I-75 send this message to millions of travelers, "ALCOHOL AND DRUGS KILL - JUST SAY NO". A billboard in Tampa, Florida reads, "MORE PEOPLE ARE KILLED BY SHOTS THAN BULLETS". The sponsors of these messages have first-hand experience with their clients. They usually find them in hospitals or funeral homes and it ain't a fun time.

Don't be fooled - anyone can become a problem drinker or an alcoholic by social drinking. It all begins with the first drink. You say, "But you must be mistaken. I'm a crusader against drugs, and even have a sticker on my car that reads "SAY NO TO DRUGS". That's great, but you should be against all drugs. One of the most devastating drugs is alcohol. Beer is especially dangerous, because most people consider it harmless. Many still believe they can drink socially and it's no big deal. Sad to say, some will end up in a hospital or funeral home. Tragically, they may take someone with them, as did the drunk driver who killed five teenagers and himself. Instead of "GET HIGH - GET STUPID - GET AIDS". Let's "GET SMART - GET WISE - GET LIFE."

There is a simple answer. If you drink or do drugs, QUIT! STOP! If you are offered a drink or drug, JUST SAY NO. It takes a REAL teen, man or woman to say "NO" but that's really LIVING LIFE WITH A CAPITAL "L".

# You Are What You Are

Did you ever hear of CACKLING NONSENSE? That's what a scraggly sparrow called some birds trying to decide who was the happiest bird. The birds lived in a wooded glen. There were seeds and nuts everywhere and enough insects and worms to carpet a forest floor. "But who is the happiest bird?" demanded the owl, "I'm happy" trilled the robin, "but not that happy. I wish I could soar like the eagle."

"I can really wing it," agreed the eagle, "but I think I'd be much happier if I could look like the graceful swan."

"You're all wet," pointed out the swan. "For my part, I'd really be happy if I had the fan and colorful feathers of the peacock."

"You're all cackling nonsense," exclaimed the scraggly sparrow. "Use your little brains. Think! YOU ARE WHAT YOU ARE, NO MORE. You can't be another bird. Be happy you are you." (From *Printopics*)

ENVY IS LIKE A GREEN-EYED MONSTER. It will eat you up and spit you out. Most of us believe we would be happier if we looked better, did better, had better, won the lottery, were the top-dog and got our heart's desire. The scraggly sparrow would call that cackling nonsense. He would say, "USE YOUR BIRD BRAIN, ACCEPT WHAT GOD HAS GIVEN YOU. FORGET ENVY. BE HAPPY YOU ARE YOU, AND BE THE BEST YOU CAN BE WITH GOD'S HELP."

# Peace of Mind Happiness

Are you happy? I don't mean "Ha-Ha" happy. I mean peace of mind happiness - soft pillow sleep, like a baby sleeping with a clear conscience.

A *Peanuts* TV cartoon scene showed Lucy saying to Snoopy, "I want to be first." The next scene shows Lucy saying, "I represent the beauty and majesty of Christmas." In the following scene Lucy is saying emphatically, "But I still want to be first." Lucy chose to be self-centered so her choice only brought sadness and unhappiness.

Did you hear about the man who was being ridden out of town on a rail by the townspeople? The man said, "If it wasn't for the honor of the ride, I'd just as soon walk." This man's positive attitude didn't change his ride, but it at least made it bearable.

Attitude determines happiness, not things and possessions. If you are a grouch, STOP GROUCHING! If a complainer, STOP COMPLAINING! If you are a hater, STOP HATING! If you are jealous, STOP BEING JEALOUS! Keep a smile in your heart and on your face, even if you are riding a rail. There are rails you will have to ride as long as you dwell on this planet. The disciple Paul expressed it best, "I have learned the secret of being content in every situation, whether well fed or hungry, whether living in plenty or in want. I can do everything through Christ who gives me strength." Kousin Zeke sez, "EVEN IF YOU HALF-WAY TRY WHAT PAUL SAID, THEN FINDING HAPPINESS AIN'T NO PROBLEM."

# Don't Underestimate Your Worth

Does it ever cross your mind?  I'm not really too good at anything and I guess you could call me a no talent person.  I honestly try, but just can't cut it!

Every Christmas season you and I are blessed by the words and music of *White Christmas*. The movie *White Christmas* has become a TV Christmas tradition.  On special patriotic occasions, worship services, events, and holidays, we are inspired by *God Bless America*. At Easter, we are filled with joy and our hearts are lifted up with happiness as we listen to the melody of *Easter Parade*.  We are reminded of the true meaning of Easter.

These songs are only three of over 1,000 songs written by a man who immigrated from Russia to America as a small boy.  He had no education and no musical training.  He wrote every song in the key of "F."  His name was Irving Berlin and he became the most famous song writer in American history.  His songs are played daily over thousands of radio and TV stations.  He was so popular that often movie theaters would put his name over the name of the movie on the marquee.

When you begin to ponder what you can't do and how much talent you don't have, think about Irving Berlin.  REMEMBER with a truck load of SINCERE EFFORT and a DAB OF GOD-GIVEN FAITH you can do anything you set your mind to.

*Kousin Zeke sez:*
*"You can be somebody 'cause God don't make nobodies!"*

# Bite Your Tongue

Did you ever say something and were so ashamed you would almost give your right arm to take back your words? I did. I learned a lesson that spared me from a life-time bundle of garbage talk for me and others.

As a teenager, I worked in a large grocery store. The manager, Mr. Oliver, loved me as his adopted son. On this particular day, Mr. Oliver had corrected me and I resented it. Later, I went to the barber, and as he was cutting my hair, I began to spout off about Mr. Oliver. I talked about how mean and hateful he was. The barber quickly put me in my place. He turned the barber chair around and staring into my face he said, "Jack, suppose I told Mr. Oliver exactly what you just told me?" Believe me I was so ashamed I could have walked under the door sill. I'm so thankful Mr. Oliver was never told what I had said. I learned a lesson about biting my tongue early in life from a barber who had enough sense to see through my foolish talk and tell me the truth.

What's the lesson I learned and we all need to learn? IF YOU CAN'T SAY SOMETHING GOOD ABOUT OTHERS, SAY NOTHING. If we can live by this motto, we can prevent more heartaches, destroyed friendships and reputations than you can shake a stick at. If necessary, put a chain on your tongue and when gossip and trash talk begins to spill out, PULL IT.

A wise man, Simon Peter, gave some good advice 2,000 years ago; "GET RID OF FEELINGS OF HATRED. DON'T JUST PRETEND TO BE GOOD. STOP BEING DISHONEST AND TALKING ABOUT OTHERS BEHIND THEIR BACKS." Kousin Zeke sez, "That shore am good advice, but it ain't worth DOODLY SQUAT if we don't practice it. Now am a good time to begin practicing!"

# Johnny, the Party Guy

When you think about it, life can dish out some strange and weird twists. My name is Johnny and I have five brothers. My family is what you might call good-time or party-time boys. In our community, we run with the country club set as well as the good ol' country crowd. In reality, we are chums with both the up & outers and the down & outers. I do have to admit, some Moms and Dads of our friends don't want us to buddy with their kids. They discourage their kids from running with me and my brothers. In some ways, I can't blame them.

Me and my brothers are party people. We go for the good times. You can find us at all kinds of occasions, special and not so special. Those who know us make it a point to see that we are their guests, especially at sports events. Too often, more than I like to admit, tragedies occur that transform our fun-times into gloom-times. I remember the time I was riding in a car with two of my pals. We hit another car head on, traveling over 80 miles an hour. My two buddies were killed and the rescue teams found me in the lap of one of the dead teens. I heard the officers talking and one said, "I'm not surprised." Another time I was in Key West riding with a buddy in his car and he was driving. He hit an 11-year old boy who was riding his bike and dragged him over a mile. You should have heard the screams of the people along the highway who witnessed the scene.

But parents have every right to question their children and family when they desire to be a bosom buddy with me. You see, I'm responsible for people being robbed, injured, killed, divorced, molested, jailed, fired and many other forms of suffering. Oh! I apologize, I forgot to tell you that my name is Johnny Six Pack.

# Obsessed With Exercise?

Do you exercise?  Do you own some type of exercise gear?  Have you been bombarded by TV ads?  Most ads attempt to convince us that their exerciser is the best and will help us lose weight, look and feel better, be healthier and live longer.  One ad promises to make a lifestyle change in 90 days, if you purchase their products.

I believe everyone needs to have a regular exercise routine that fits their physical needs and age.  I lift weights and ride a stationary bike.  Thus far, my wife and I have ridden the bike over 5,000 miles.  I walk up stairs instead of taking the elevator, whenever possible. The sad note is that many people become so obsessed with their exercise routine that it becomes their number one priority, even before their family and responsibilities.

Our goal should be to strive for a balanced life: physically, mentally and spiritually.  Everyone possesses a body, mind and soul.  This is best explained by what a lady told me, "As I went into the YMCA, I read a sign that said, IF YOU REALLY WANT TO GIVE YOUR HEART A WORK-OUT, LIFT SOMEBODY UP SPIRITUALLY, PHYSICALLY AND EMOTIONALLY."  The purpose of exercise is to make us physically fit to serve others and to MAKE A DIFFERENCE IN THIS WORLD.  If we do it just to look better, WE FAIL.  Let's choose to make a difference.  I promise you will feel and look better.  You will have a strong, happy heart, and a smile on your face to pass on to others.

# For Fun or Fish?

Kousin Zeke tells me, "I sure do like to fish. Oh, I ain't no expert. Guess you would say I know what fishes likes to nibble on, and how to get the fishes to like 'em."

"Let me tell you what happened one hot summer day. You see, I was fishin' at Uncle Joe's pond, a real good fishin' hole. Three boys drives up in a fancy sports car. When those boys pile out of that car, I ain't never seen such fanciful fishin' paraphernalia in my life! I can't even imagine what it would be to own such rods and reels. Oh well, I can't complain 'cause I do pretty good with my ol' cane pole. I know them boys from school and town, sorta. We live in the same town, you could say, but on different sides of the tracks.

"While trying to fish, them three boys talked, laughed, told jokes and made noises. They did everything 'cept catch fish. Meanwhile, I was catchin' fish one after another. Finally, one of 'em named Carl came over and in disgust said, 'Zeke, how come you're catching fish and we're not?' All I know is, YOU'RE FISHIN' FOR FUN AND I'M FISHIN' FOR FISH. Carl, I believe in fun, but in this life there is a time for fun and a time to mean business. When those fish hit the frying pan at home, Mama knows I meant business today."

# RX For Sleep

Having difficulty sleeping?  Going to sleep and waking up in the middle of the night?
Do you want to remove stress and worry from your mind?  Most of us do.  Here is a
tried and proven prescription.  It does not require a pill or drug.  It is the words of a
1911 hymn.  If you honestly and sincerely make these words your prayer, it will clean
out any cobwebs and sins in your life.  This will provide you with comfort, peace of
mind and heart.  Make this a daily habit and you can sleep like a baby.  THIS IS A
HOUSE-CLEANING EVERYONE NEEDS.  Now ain't that a good and happy thought?

## An Evening Prayer*

*If I have wounded any soul today, If I have caused one foot to go astray,
If I have walked in my own will-ful way, Dear Lord, for-give!*

*If I have uttered idle words in vain, If I have turned aside want or pain,
Lest I myself shall suffer thru the strain, Dear lord, for-give!*

*If I have been perverse, or hard or cold, If I have longed for shelter in Thy fold,
When Thou hast given me a fort to hold, Dear Lord, for-give.*

*Forgive the sins I have confessed to Thee; Forgive the secret I do not want to see;
O guide me, love me, and my keeper be, Dear Lord, for-give.*

                                                    A-men.

*Copyright 1911 by Charles H. Gabriel
From the Cokesbury Worship Hymnal

# Talkin' Trash

Steve Allen, famous comedian of movie, TV and radio said, "They just don't make jokes like they used to. I'm fed up with performers who use vulgar language to get a laugh. We laughed at Sid Caesar, Jackie Gleason, Red Skelton and many other wonderful comedians because they were funny." Most comedians today apparently believe that only off-color jokes can produce laughs and entertainment. I was in the Navy, so there isn't much I haven't heard, but today's humor is often objectionable entertainment and in poor taste.

This problem is evident in the multitudes today, not just comedians. Are you familiar with "Garbage In, Garbage Out?" If we watch and listen to garbage, then eventually we will begin to use vile language as well!

Steve Allen suggested that the time has come to poll the American people to determine what percentage of them like the constant daily barrage of vile language used in the movies, TV and by today's comedians. A poll is a five star idea, but there is an on-going poll that is as plain as the nose on your face. It is the millions of people who regularly watch shows like Lucy, Bill Cosby, Doris Day, Andy Griffith, Dick Van Dyke, and Carol Burnett. They know that famous comedians do not need barnyard filth to be funny!

A man named Paul told us 2,000 years ago how to get rid of garbage. He said "Think on the things that are true, honest, just, pure, lovely and of good report. For God has not called us to be dirty-minded and full of lust, but to be holy and clean." Kousin Zeke sez, "Man, that am some good advice to practice! If you do, you'll be happier and even your friends will begin to like you again. How 'bout we do it together?"

# Friendliness Epidemic

Did you ever wake up with a pounding headache, a high fever, perspiring like you'd been thrown in a swimming pool, every bone aching, sore from head to toe and so miserable you wondered if you could survive another day?  You ask yourself if there is any pill or medicine that will give even a moment of relief, while silently thinking, "If I felt any worse I'd be dead and wondering what fatal disease I caught."

Guess What????  You will live, and you will get better, 'cause you got the flu. You won't die from it, but sometimes you wouldn't mind if you did.  It is very contagious - every year newspaper headlines warn the public about the flu bug epidemic.  Although the flu is bad and highly contagious, hatred, envy, jealousy, anger and greed are even worse.  But there is a way to respond to these nasty emotions. Try being friendly!

We can catch and spread the friendly epidemic.  Did you realize that FRIENDLINESS and courtesy are highly infectious and easily given to others? Since this is true, let's BEGIN a world-wide friendliness epidemic.  How?  Make a genuine effort to be friendly to strangers, neighbors, friends and family every day.  If you see someone without a smile, give them yours.  You'll be amazed at how fast the friendly bug will spread.

As Nike says,  "Just Do It."  Pass the friendly bug at home, work and play.  Kousin Zeke sez, "Now that's an epidemic that's long overdue!"

# No More Doom and Gloom

Is your glass half full or half empty? Will it be a good day or a rotten day? I'm here to tell you, my glass is half full and it's going to be a great day! Do you know why? Because I'm a born optimist. I always look on the sunshiny side of life. If you tell me how gloomy and rotten life is, I will spend the next 24 hours telling you how good it can be.

In a *Readers Digest* article called "Our Plague of Pessimism," the writer said, "The most deadly plague menacing children today is not AIDS, gang violence or teen pregnancy — it's the plague of pessimism. Millions of teens are feeling their patience, faith and hope challenged and undermined. Some of the culprits are too much TV, violence, sex, rude behavior, and bad news media. Killing is covered and kindness ignored. Trash talk TV and radio shows abound. Last, but certainly not least, is the poor role models of adults, especially parents."

What will it take for optimism to replace pessimism in our land? Adults and teens who no longer require popularity and applause to succeed and who live by faith and integrity. An African pastor said it best, "We need adults and teens who cannot be compromised, detoured, lured away, deluded, turned back or delayed. Will not flinch in the face of sacrifice, negotiate at the table of the enemy, ponder at the pool of popularity or meander in the maze of mediocrity." Kousin Zeke sez, "If we halfway do what this pastor said, we no longer will have to dwell in the land of doom and gloom. Nobody is gonna put doom and gloom on me, 'cause my maker is in charge of the sunshine factory." What about you?

# A Bundle of Courage

Does the name Raoul Wallenberg mean anything to you?  For most people it doesn't, but for 100,000 Jews it does. Raoul, a Swedish Protestant, saved them from Hitler's furnaces. He heard their distress cries and they became his mission.  Lauded as a shining light in a dark and torturous world, Raoul proved that one person can make a difference.  The Swedish Parliament said, "He was a glowing torch in total darkness." A writer said,  "I know some brittle people; illness, bad luck, and disappointment could crack them into brittle pieces like dried leaves, never to recover.  I also know some people who can rebound, bruised but safe, from a full-force hurricane."

Regardless of the difficulties we may encounter, there is within almost every person a bundle of courage waiting to be released.  You don't have to be a Rocket Scientist to realize that millions of people are groping in darkness and searching for some kind of light. If we make ourselves available, God will place groping, stumbling people in our paths as he did for Raoul Wallenberg.  We then have the privilege of pointing them to the true light, Jesus Christ.  We are not the light, only a reflection of the light.

Kousin Zeke sez, "If we is gonna be a light reflector, time is important.  All we own is one second at a time; not a year, month or even a day.  Guess what?  A second just passed me by, but thank God another second is coming that will let me use my little bit of courage to help a groping pilgrim.  Now that is some happy thought!"

*Treasure your seconds!*

# Playing the Blame Game

Did you ever read the story of four strange people?  The four were named EVERYBODY, SOMEBODY, ANYBODY and NOBODY. There was an important job to be done and EVERYBODY was sure that SOMEBODY would do it.  ANYBODY could have done it, but NOBODY did it.  SOMEBODY got angry about that, because it was EVERYBODY's job.  EVERYBODY thought ANYBODY could do it, but EVERYBODY blamed SOMEBODY when NOBODY did what ANYBODY could have done.  Who do we blame, Uncle Peter or Cousin Sue?

A professional athlete blamed his family for his poor play, until he realized he was to blame.  An ex-husband told his former wife how fat and ugly she was, when in reality she was slim and beautiful.  He was trying to get relief from the guilt of deserting his wife and children.

We must be careful lest we blame others when we are at fault.  Flip Wilson, the comedian, had a pet saying: "The Devil made me do it."  Believe me, you and I are responsible for our actions and cannot go through life blaming others.  Kousin Zeke sez, "That's what you call HAVING A PITY PARTY and that ain't no party you want to mingle in.  The host at the PITY PARTY is a MEBODY.  Mebody is a word I thunk up. If you don't know who a mebody is, see who peeks back in a mirror."

Regardless of how we have been mistreated, neglected or put-down, if we play the BLAME GAME, we lose.  It would help if we:

- *Stopped blaming others*
- *Prayed for them*
- *Asked for forgiveness*

Heed the advice of Paul, writing to some friends who had been mistreated, "Be kind to each other, tenderhearted, forgiving one another, just as God has forgiven you, because you belong to Christ."

*If you want to be a genuine somebody,*
*then practice this advice!*

# The Right Decision

Jim is a pharmaceutical salesman, a family man with three children.  His sales territory is from Miami to Key West.  One morning, after kissing his wife good-bye, he began to wonder what surprises would await him on this trip.  He remembered many accidents on the Seven Mile Bridge, but the trip down to the Keys was uneventful.  It was the experience on the return trip that was more than he could ever imagine!

On the way back to Miami, he decided to stop and spend the night at a motel.  As he was relaxing around the pool, a stranger walked up and said, "Sir may I speak with you for a moment?"  Jim said, "Yes, of course, please sit down."  The man said in a nervous tone, "Can our conversation be confidential?"  Jim said, "I don't know why it can't."  The stranger continued, "Then can we talk in the lobby?"  "I guess so," Jim replied.

When they sat down at a table in an isolated corner of the lobby, the man said, "You don't know me, but I know a lot about you."  Then he took out an envelope and in a soft whisper said, "This contains $5,000.  It can be yours each week if you just do one thing — leave the doors of your van open once a week.  That's it, no strings."  Then Jim's mind began to play tricks on him, "so much money - no strings - bills paid - all the goodies we ever wanted," he thought.  Then Jim's mind got into first gear.  He remembered his wife, children, his example and responsibility before others.  Jim looked the man in the face and said, "THANKS, BUT NO THANKS."  When the man left, Jim looked upward with his eyes closed and said, "Thank you, and thanks for parents who taught me right from wrong and how to make the right decisions."

# The Boo Bug

Did you know that there is a widespread, uncontrollable Boo Epidemic in America? Did I misspell Flu for Boo? No, I'm writing about the BOO BUG that is running rampant in stadiums all over America. The BOO BUG attacks sports teams, coaches and officials. It is a sickening virus for visiting teams, but it also attacks the home team and players. One doctor told me the Bug is extremely contagious. He was upset because the public is doing nothing to control the disease. The doctor said, "The BOO BUG can be transmitted just by sitting next to someone who has it."

Booers say, "I don't care what you did for me last year, yesterday, or what you promise for tomorrow. What can you do for me today, right now? All we want is a winner." If you ask a BOO BUG why they boo, many say, "I paid for the ticket and I have a right to boo, or be rude and arrogant, if I choose." That is debatable. I have never read on any ticket where you have permission to be rude, profane or to spit out filth. I realize there are exceptions, but those I hear put common sense decency and behavior on the back burner. Ask yourself if you would like to be booed. Where does "Do Unto Others" fit in? It ain't no joking matter!

Some characteristics of BOO BUGS:

- *Fair-weather fans*
- *Poor sports and losers*
- *Often hateful and insulting*

If you are infected with the BOO BUG, ask yourself if you can play as well or better than the professional. Let me answer it for you, YOU CAN'T. It's sad to say, but you will discover BOO BUGS in every day events, not just sports. Kousin Zeke sez, "The best medicine for the BOO BUG is a big dose of COMMON SENSE DECENCY. The best cure? DON'T BOO!"

# Are You Fairly Honest?

Do you realize that stealing is a way of life for many people?  To them it's no big deal.
I was in a department store, and looked down and there was an empty pair of ladies'
slippers.  How come?  Some lady decided to borrow a new pair — steal them that is.
It is unbelievable, but some ladies selling Girl Scout cookies were robbed.  Ask any
store manager what is his worse problem and he will sadly tell you, SHOPLIFTING and
STEALING.  Today, stealing is not simply a problem, it's an epidemic.

USA *Today* had this headline, "A PUSH TO TEACH ETHICS AND ABCs." This study by
the American Association of School Administration asked that RESPONSIBILITY,
REASONING, RESPECT and ETHICS SHOULD PERMEATE THE ENTIRE SCHOOL
PROCESS.  If we lose it in the schools, we will lose the AMERICAN DREAM.

A mother told me, "My son would buy any stolen item.  He said 'It's no big deal' until
he was robbed of his precious goodies.  Then his attitude changed and he said, 'I never
realized what it did to the victims.''  The thief's final victim is him/herself.  Suppose
you stole a penny,  pencil or stamp.  Is that stealing?  Are you a thief?  Yep, you're
a crook.  You can't be "fairly" honest.  Some FAIRLY HONEST people will disagree and
say, "I'm not really dishonest.  I'm a good person and a responsible citizen.  Let me
toss you a question - can a woman be "fairly" pregnant?  I didn't mean to upset you,
just thought I'd ask.

Kousin Zeke sez, "Stealing is a sin.  If you steal, you deserve jail.  Don't fuss at me,
'cause I don't make the rules!  Moses and Jesus make the rules.  You could wait and
ask them on Judgment Day.  If I wuz you, I'd check it out before, 'cause you better know
the PROPER and PRECISE answers when your NUMBER POPS UP. "

# Tales of a Golf Ball

Me, I'm just a golf ball covered with small dimples. My owner, Joe, hits me with a golf club. He bought me at a yard sale for 75¢, never realizing that I could talk. Joe is a family man, community leader, and to most people, a regular guy. Remember, I am not a person, but a golf ball who wants to tell about my owner, Joe. I think he has some odd and strange habits, but let me tell you and you decide.

In golf, you win with the lowest score. Once I was in a sand trap. Joe hit me and I only moved five inches - but it counts as a stroke. No problem for Joe... his total score on that hole was five. When asked his score, he said "I had a four." I guess he flunked math. Another time I was in high grass, hidden from his partners. Joe stepped on me, and then nudged me into a clear spot with his foot. He hollered to his pals "Guess what? I landed in a clear spot and saved a stroke!"

Joe bragged about how good he was at putting. I soon learned why. Once, I was five feet from the hole when he picked me up, wiped me off and put me back down on the green. Guess what? Now I was only four feet from the hole. He must be near-sighted.

I know the rules of golf, but old Joe had his own rules about golf and life. Maybe that ís the way humans act and think today. Once Joe carried me home, took me out of his pocket and set me on his dresser. I hear Joe lecturing his children, "You must never lie or cheat in this house." I thought, but didn't say, "Hey Joe, how 'bout the GOLF COURSE?" Thank the Lord, Joe is not a golf ball like me. He would bring shame to all golf balls. I forgot to tell you the nickname given Joe by his partners is "FAIRLY HONEST JOE."

*If you lose integrity, you lose,*
*even if you win!*

# Deadbeat Dads

What is a Deadbeat Dad? A Dad who fathers children, divorces, or leaves his wife and makes little or no effort to pay child support or alimony. Meanwhile, the wife struggles to pay the bills and provide the necessary essentials for herself and their children.

Most "Good Ol' Deadbeat Dads" do their own thing, whatever that is; father more children, find a live-in, get married, live high on the hog, eat, drink, be merry, complain, lie and swear they can't afford to pay child support. Meanwhile, the wife has to make a valiant attempt by every means possible to get even token support for the children.

Why must wives of Deadbeat Dads experience such a hassle to survive? Because trifling, no-good dads are irresponsible and expect the state or others to pick up their tab. Thank God, the Governor of Florida is getting tough on Deadbeat Dads. He said, "If you are a deadbeat, we are coming after you. And we're going to do it by using every avenue open to us to make you pay."

An editorial in the *Tampa Tribune* hit the nail on the head. "It is past time to stop insulating the Deadbeat Dads from the consequences of their profligate action toward children and wives. What they have done is a terrible thing. Their children are suffering because of it. And the rest of society must endure the crime and chaos committed in schools by confused children, hurt and deprived from their situation." Other consequences of their misguided ways will emerge to hurt society. If you doubt it, read or listen to the daily news.

It is time Deadbeat Dads are tracked down and compelled to pick up their tabs and responsibilities. I don't know much about judgment, but I know some wives who will gladly toss their Deadbeats in jail and throw the key away. I would applaud their decision. Jesus didn't mind telling it like it is when it came to Deadbeats. He said, "If anyone harms one of these little children, it would be better for him that a large rock were tied to his neck and he was thrown into the sea."

If this article bugs or upsets you, you are probably a Deadbeat Dad, or contemplating becoming one.

# Riding Shotgun

A teenager shouts above all other voices, "I get to ride Shotgun!" Teens use this old stagecoach days expression when piling into a car. Riding shotgun is to sit in the best seat by the window. The problem is that too many kids spend much of their lives trying to ride shotgun and be Number One. There is nothing wrong with being Number One, unless our motives are for me, mine and ours.

If you doubt it, ask the coach with a team of shotgun riders and crybabies — each pouting because they can't be a star. Ask the kicker with over 100 perfect kicks or the pitcher with a no-hitter, believing they are the elite and failing to understand their record is a team effort. If just one team member misses an assignment, their record can slip down the drain.

The thorn of discontent in big league sports, little league sports, the work-place, or politics is: "IF YOU DON'T DO IT MY WAY, I'LL TAKE MY BALL AND GO HOME." One NFL coach said, "We don't have the quality players of other teams, but we play together as a team and win." Irving Fryar, a Miami Dolphin football player, expressed it best after scoring four touchdowns. Pointing his fingers toward his chest, while shaking his head to indicate, "No, it is not me," then pointing upward to denote "victory is never achieved alone."

Too many of us squander our lives listening for applause and thanks, when we should be asking, "What can I do to help?" One unquestionable fact:

> *"With teamwork you can achieve success and happiness,*
> *thereby avoiding the pain and hurt of the ME FIRST syndrome."*

# Coping With Agitators

Do you know, work with, or have contact with someone who bugs you, is a constant source of irritation and literally drives you up a wall? Joyce Landorf calls these people IRREGULAR PERSONS. I call them AGITATORS. Joyce says, "These people are the ones who have the knack of wounding you every time you see them. They make thoughtless remarks, ruin your day, and keep your emotions in constant turmoil. These people have negative personalities. You can't reason, depend or expect any support from them." You can expect criticism and fault-finding. Someone said, "An agitator can see more shortcomings through a keyhole than most through an open door." They can see the worst and best. Agitators are in every walk of life. You will find them where you work, play and live. Like it or not, you have to endure, tolerate, and live with them, unless you crawl into a ground-hog hole. I've seen the time when I would prefer to be in the hole with the ground-hog! The problem is how to cope, survive and learn to live with Agitators. It ain't easy. It takes all the patience, love and forgiveness you can store up or stockpile.

A suggestion for coping with an agitator is to try to understand why he or she behaves in such a detestable manner. Some never improve, and as the farmer says, "they gets worser." Remember, you are not their dart board, they usually treat others the same way. You must alter your attitude and not permit them to control or dominate you. A word of caution — beware of anger! Anger is a virus that affects the attitude and spirit. Don't make hateful and harsh remarks. Always keep your relationships with others and God open, and your forgiveness up-to-date. Don't forget, you have two holes in your head, GARBAGE IN and GARBAGE OUT. You must choose to free your mind of negative garbage.

*The choice is yours.*
*As difficult as it is, love and pray for the Agitator.*

# The Worry-Go-Round

Are you on a Worry-Go-Round? Is your mind overwhelmed by fears and worries - churning 24 hours a day seeking solutions? Proverbs 3:5,6 has the PRESCRIPTION FOR WORRY. God promises I WILL DIRECT YOUR LIFE if you follow this prescription:

1. Trust Your Worry to God - without reservation
2. Do Not Meddle
3. Do God's Will

It's odd. Some people have every cause to worry, but they don't. Others have no logical reason to worry, but worry incessantly.

Let me share a method that has given peace of mind to thousands and will help you to get off the Worry-Go-Round. A television auctioneer illustrated the method best, as he spouted out his auctioneers lingo, he periodically said "talk to this ol' boy." Here's how I apply this phrase; when I have a nagging worry that continually robs me of joy and peace, I talk to this ol' boy, Jack. I say to myself, "Jack, are you going to give God your worry or are you going to continue to carry it by yourself?" When I find myself trying to carry it alone, I say, "No, God, it's yours again." Then I intentionally begin to count my blessings, one by one. When the worry pops back into my mind, and it will, I say "God, it's yours again." Then I immediately begin to recount my blessings. If you can trust your worry to God for one minute, then you can trust him for two minutes. Eventually, you will be able to trust for ten minutes, hours, even days. Doing this will clear your mind of mental fatigue and give you peace.

At first, turning your worries over to God will be difficult, but with practice you will cease thinking (meddling) and do more trusting. Little by little, each day, you will make progress and it will be easier to trust and more difficult to worry (meddle.)

# I Mint To....

Do you like mints?  I love mints.  Recently, I coughed a couple of times and someone gave me a mint.  I asked, "Is this a cough drop?"  She replied, "No, it's a caramel mint, but it will help your cough."  She didn't know it, but caramel is my very favorite mint.

There are some mints that I don't like, because they do more harm than good.  A verse from a poem talks about some harmful mints:

> I MINT *to share my new life with you,*
> *But time* I *spent doing other things.*
> I MINT *to tell you about my Savior — but!*

Kousin Zeke sez, "Most of us ain't mean, we just too full of procrastination.  We have good intentions, but the way I hear it, the road to Hell is paved with good intentions and "mints."  I mint to help a friend, give to the hungry, visit a shut-in, write a thank you letter, be kinder to my family, clean up my language and change my bad habits, BUT..."

Let's decide this moment to stop saying what we are going to do, and do what we ought to do.  It ain't no big complication.

*Just stop the "mints" and start the "do's!"*

# Share A Smileshine

Do you realize that you possess something that 99 out of 100 people want and need? It's something that makes the sad glad and the depressed laugh. I was checking out of the Tampa General Hospital parking garage and the lady attendant said with a radiant smile, "How are you today, darlin'?" I said, "Your smile is a blessing to all the hurting people coming to the hospital." She replied, "God gave me this smile to give to others." You could call it SMILESHINE.

SMILES are like Tender Loving Hugs (TLH). There are no batteries to wear out, no monthly payments and they are inflation proof and theft proof. Do you give away GLOOM-SHINE or SMILESHINE? You may say, "Jack, you just don't know how bad I have it. It can't get any worse." Kousin Zeke would say, "There is always somebody worser off than you. Just take a peek and someone will cross your path needing a SMILESHINE."

Be a copy-cat like the parking attendant. Realize that God gave you smiles to give to a friend, stranger, family member or whoever may need SMILESHINE to soothe aching hurts. If you see someone without a smile, give them yours. You'll be happily surprised at how many smiles will be thrown back at you. Believe me, it's better than pills.

# Master Carpenter Remodels Hypocrites

Do you know a hypocrite?  Would you recognize one if you saw one?  Is it possible you are a hypocrite?

A pastor had just been assigned to a church in a new community and was visited by a local man.  The man said, "Pastor, I've lived all my life in this community and you need to know that most of the people here are hypocrites and phonies.  If I were you, I would kick them out of the church."  The pastor paused for a moment and said, "Maybe you are right, I will kick them out."  The man interrupted the pastor and said, "You're really gonna do that?"  "Oh yes," the pastor replied, "just as soon as the hospitals kick out all their sick and injured."  The man in the story is like so many self-made hypocrites. He can explain and recite the faults of others 'til doomsday.  Bona fide hypocrites do not consider themselves hypocrites because they are convinced that they are the elected number one judge of others.  If you doubt it, just ask them.

Kousin Zeke sez, "My Lord tells me, why worry about a speck in the eye of a brother when you have a two-by-four in your own?  Hypocrite!  First get rid of the two-by-four, then you can see to help your brother."  I wonder what a hypocrite sees when they look in the mirror?

Perhaps the sawdust in our eyes is from the wood chips of jealousy, hatred and criticism.  If so, call on the MASTER CARPENTER and let him remove the rotten two-by-fours.  Then we can see to pass on Love instead of Hurts.  Kousin Zeke sez,

*"Now that's my kind of thinking.*
*Let's start remodeling today!"*

# Three Gates of Gold

Are you tempted to reveal foolish tales told to you, or do you let them pass?  Too often we hear, "Have you heard the latest?  Can you keep a secret?  Do you know about Susie Q and Jimbo, too?  I can't believe what Janie told me, so much juicy gossip and trash, so it must be true. Please don't tell anyone I told you because it was told to me in the strictest confidence. But I know I can trust you, right?"

A poem said it best:

> *Three gates of gold*
> *a foolish tale should pass*
> *before we speak about someone else*:
> *First - Is it true?*
> *Second - Is it needful?*
> *Third - Is it kind?*

If our tale can pass these three gates, we can reveal, without fear and concern, what the results will be.  Then we will be happier and so will Susie Q and Jimbo.

# Make Time to Care

It is said that this is the 17 second generation. A hotel chain claims a guest check-in takes 30 seconds. A machine provides a key, prints directions to the room, and activates the phone, air conditioning and lighting. I figger the only personal touch a guest will receive is a "pay-up", "hi" and "bye". The average resume is read for 22 seconds. If you desperately needed a job to pay your bills and feed your family, but the resume you sent was only glanced at for 22 seconds, you would be upset.

Sam Walton of WalMart discovered the secret to success when other stores were failing. He placed greeters at every door just to welcome customers. That idea wouldn't fare too well with computerized, 17 second nerds, but it sure helped make WalMart.

A businessman asked me if I knew who were his most important employees. He said his most important employees were those parking cars.

In the "Good Samaritan" parable, the man robbed and beaten was bypassed by the 17 second do-gooders. They had to check their computers, E-Mail, on-line, out-lined, scanned and banned. Somewhere lost in their computers was TENDER LOVING CARE. The Good Samaritan took time to share love and concern.

Kousin Zeke sez, "It don't make no good sense that our common sense is computerized and homogenized by the 17 second generation." What should we do?

*Make time, and take time, to be a ray of hope*
*to those in their darkest hours.*

# Forgiveness: It Ain't No Fun, But It Must Be Done

Do you know the most difficult decision most of us have to make?  The decision to forgive others, whether they are right or wrong.  It ain't no fun, it ain't easy, but it must be done.  When we can't forgive, it is hazardous to our total well-being.
Forgiveness brings peace and often replaces pills and medical bills.  When we harbor resentments and find it difficult to forgive others, we say "why me?" with thoughts of revenge and pay-back.  Have you been there?  Are you there now?

Suppose someone, let's call him Juston, tells a vicious lie about you.  Suddenly anger causes you to lash out verbally with hatred.  What does this do to your relationship with Juston?  It breaks your relationship with Juston and with God.  Three steps you must take to restore those relationships:

1. You must restore your relationship with God.  How?  Ask God to forgive you (1 John 1:9).
2. You must forgive Juston, right or wrong.  Remember how Juston told a vicious lie about you?  That was wrong, but you were wrong when you began to spit out your own verbal hatred.  So how is it possible to forgive and be forgiven?  Read on.........
3. Begin to pray for Juston.  This may be the most difficult thing you have ever done.

Your first prayer may be short (and probably not sweet) but continue to pray every day until an attitude of compassion creeps into your prayers.  Remember, you are not responsible for Juston's spiritual response; God will take care of that.  Just be certain your prayers are spiced with sincere forgiveness and love.  Don't forget, it ain't no fun, but it must be done.  The rewards?  Quietness of Heart and Mind.

*(Read Matthew 5:43 - 48; 18:21,22  Collossians 3:13)*

# The Worry Jar

According to an old fable, the devil decided to sell some of his well-worn tools. On sale and display were some repulsive utensils, including lying, hatred, gossip and jealousy. On a shelf, set apart from the others, was a harmless looking tool with a high price tag. "What's this?" someone asked. "That's discouragement," Satan replied, "it's one of my most effective tools. With it, I can fill hearts with discouragement and worries."

What can we do about worry? Worry has no favorites. You will be faced with your worst enemy, your thinking, as your mind schemes night and day trying to solve your problems. Kousin Zeke sez, "The old devil is a smart one. 'Bout the time you think you ain't got no worries, he will saddle you with a bunch of hogwash."

Are there any solutions for worry? Mrs. Deanna Dean uses THE WORRY JAR. She says, "For more than 20 years, my parents and I have used THE WORRY JAR and it has never failed to ease my mind. Whenever one of us has a worry, we jot it down on a piece of paper and drop it into the jar. Before bed that evening, we ask God to take our worries and give us peace. When we clean out the jar, we're always happily surprised to see how many worries never materialize and how trivial most were." Stop living on Wits-End Corner and trust yourself and all your cares to Christ. Change your thinking and begin to count your many blessings. Try THE WORRY JAR. Little by little you will make headway. It will be easier to trust and more difficult to worry.

# Be a Mega Cool Servant

I complimented a funeral director about the kindly manner in which he comforted a bereaved family.  His reply shocked me.  He said,  I value your remarks, but our corporate office in another state only wants to know HOW MUCH MONEY WE MADE."  The trend today is let's go PRIME TIME.  As a 10 year old said on TV, "Be Mega Cool."  Be the biggest, have the most, and trample anyone who hinders your ambition.

Car rental agency, Avis, has agreed to an $800 million purchase by two companies.  The deal will bring an end to Avis history as one of the nation's most well known employee companies.  A successful country TV network has chosen to go prime time and be big time.  They forget that their success is the result of their down-home, laid-back programming and from copying other networks.  An executive for Disney World was asked, "What is the main reason for the success of Disney World?"  I would have answered promotions and big money, but his answer surprised me.  He said "word of mouth."

Even Jesus had to deal with Prime Time followers.  Some asked to sit on his right hand, others asked to be served.  He told them, "I came to serve and not to be served."  Do you want a life changing experience?  Then take Kousin Zeke's suggestion, "Be a PRIME TIME, MEGA COOL servant.  Find someone who is hurting and put a LOVE BAND-AID on their hurt.  The cost ain't much, but your reward will be GOD-GIVEN PRIME TIME JOY."

# Be the Boss of Your Senses

Are your senses normal? According to a Readers Digest article, "If your senses are normal you can: See a small candle flame from 30 miles away on a clear dark night. Smell one drop of perfume diffused through a three room apartment. Feel the weight of a bee's wing falling on your cheek less than half an inch away.

*What bothers your senses more:*
- *If your child misses Sunday School or Public School?*
- *If your bank account is up or church giving down?*
- *If your family is in church or if there is a dent in your fender?*

Does how the toilet tissue hangs bug you? It bothered thousands of Anne Landers readers. She said, "I received one of my largest responses, much was hate mail, when I mentioned how I prefer to hang the paper." You can't blame all those upset people, since how it hangs is so critical — a matter of life and death.

Does the filth, loose sex and profanity on TV and radio bug your senses? It should. Kousin Zeke sez, "If you wants a happy and peaceful mind, take charge. Be the boss of your senses. If you lets slime garbage into your mind, slime garbage will spill out. But if you take control of your God-given senses and replace the slime garbage with godliness, righteousness and honesty, then you can boot the devil out and invite Jesus in. Now that am some happy thought!"

# Win With Class

The game is almost over. The crowd noise is deafening. The fans are in a frenzy; on their feet screaming and shouting. You can hardly hear or understand the announcer, but over the crazed screaming of the crowd he shouts, "Just 30 seconds left, 20 seconds, 10 seconds. The game is over and we won, we won, we're the champs, we're the best." The crowd is going crazy. Most are holding their fingers pointing upward, saying to the world "we are number one." The fans of the opposing team have a dazed, defeated look. It's only natural, since they are the losers.

I'm always happy for the winners and want them to enjoy their victory. I know how they feel, I've been there when my team wins. Few enjoy victory more that I, especially when we are NUMBER ONE. But sad to say, many fans become jerks and become "number one" only in arrogance and self glory. They celebrate at the expense of the losers with insults. They forget that it's only a game. I hesitate to remind them that nobody wins all the time, so they, too, will experience being a loser.

If you want to be a winner, then be a winner in daily living and make a difference in this world. King Solomon, one of the wisest men, wrote in Proverbs, 18:2 "A rebel does not care about the facts. All he wants to do is yell."

Enjoy your victories, but in polite courtesy and humility. Be a class act. Kousin Zeke sez, "If most of us kept our mouths shut, others would never know how stupid we can be." This may not be a happy thought, but if it's true with you, it's well worth parading through your mind a time or two.

# Generous Giving

I'm going to make a statement that even Robert Ripley would not believe:  One of the greatest blessings of life is to be a generous giver, give to others and that's better than getting.  I can hear some of you saying, "That's a laughable statement.  Even a simpleton would know it's better to get than to give.  Ask any child if they would rather get or give, especially on birthdays or Christmas, and they would say "get".  But remember, you are an adult and not a child.

Think for a moment about the contagious joy of purchasing a gift for a friend or loved one.  The anticipation and delight of watching the person unwrap your gift.  Now that is a priceless gift money can't purchase.  If you doubt what I'm saying, take a photo of someone giving a gift instead of the person unwrapping their gift.  Note the joyful smile radiating from their face.  You will see a magic moment of happiness bursting forth.  Why?  It is more blessed to give than to receive.  That statement was made over 2,000 years ago.  The purpose of giving is not to receive, but we do receive.  That's the sure-enough meaning of Christmas - God gave the world a gift.

If you feel depressed and need a touch of JOY, find someone that is hurting.  Give of yourself, whatever it takes to soothe their hurt.  A touch of Joy will be yours.  Kousin Zeke sez, " Now, you is talking 'bout what life is all about."

*Be  stingy and miserable or generous and happy.*
*The choice is yours.*

# I've Got Humility!

Can you solve this riddle?  Name something that you can possess and never know it, yet others can recognize it immediately.  Give up?  It's HUMILITY.  Do you know anyone who has humility?  A dictionary says humility is "the state or quality of being humble or the absence of pride and self-assertion."

What humility is not:  one author said, "I wrote the best book you will ever read about humility."  What humility is:  A man asked a friend to forgive him.  The friend replied, "Certainly I'll forgive you, but I don't know what you are talking about."  The friend had completely dismissed from his mind the incident to which the man was referring.  This is authentic humility.

There is an instrument to check humility.  It's the PRONOUN BAROMETER.  Note how often someone uses "I", "mine" and "me", but be very cautious since you probably use more "I's" and "me's" than they do!  The love chapter in the Bible gives us guidelines for humility.  Genuine humility (love) is patient, kind, never jealous, envious, boastful, proud, haughty, selfish or rude.  It never demands its own way.  It is not irritable or touchy and does not hold grudges.

I'm not saying it is easy to have even a dab of sincere humility, but we can make an effort, which is a start.  Never forget, the moment you think you have it, it's gone. Kousin Zeke sez, "You'll be flabbergasted at what God can do with you if you don't care who gets the credit."

# Brown Cows and White Milk

Do you understand:

- *How a brown cow can eat green grass and then give white milk?*
- *How you can turn a TV knob and see a person talking 10,000 miles away?*
- *How small humming birds can fly thousands of miles over ocean from the U. S. to South America?*

Most people don't give doodly squat about cows giving white milk or how far humming birds can fly. Read the papers and listen to people talk and you soon discover they are trying to figger out life. They hope there is some way to get a dab of happiness and a little peace. It's sad but true, most of us try everything and every way to be happy. We try more money, gadgets, sex, fame, and status. Some steal, lie, cheat and walk over whoever, whenever.

Believe it or not, years ago, God sent his son to explain how to find peace and happiness. He said, "I want to give you peace. It's not fragile like the peace your friends and the world offers" (John 14:27). Jesus explained how to obtain peace so simply that even small children can understand how. He said, "Listen, I'm standing at your heart's door and I'm knocking. Won't you let me in? I want to help you run your life. You've already goofed up enough" (Revelation 3:20). How do you let him in? Ask God, in your own words, to forgive you of all your sins. Then invite Jesus into your heart and life. Begin to serve and obey him daily and you will discover peace and happiness.

# Real Sportsmen Don't Boo!

Let me tell you about the strangest and most unbelievable custom in America. So unreal you will not believe what I'm telling you. Imagine this scenario: A family invites some friends to their home for a special occasion and for a time of fun and pleasure. As their invited guests enter the home, the family greets them with boos, rude insults, name-calling and thrown objects. You say, "Jack, you gotta be kiddin'." Where in this cotton-pickin' world could such crude and uncivil behavior be tolerated?" Guess what? It is happening daily at sports events in stadiums and arenas all over America.

Who in their right mind could be so rude and insulting? So-called decent, law-abiding citizens, adults, youth and children. Many catch the Boo Bug and boo the opposing team, coaches, officials, and often boo their own team and coaches - forgetting that it is only a game. This is a symptom of our sick society, where all sense of sportsmanship and plain ol' common sense decency is forgotten. If you question what I am saying, go to a game, read the papers or watch TV. I realize there are millions of courteous fans, but there are thousands of model fans who begin to mimic the rude behavior of others. Never forget, when another school or team is invited to your school or city, you are the host. You are responsible for making sure that the guests are treated with kindness and courtesy.

How can we be a part of the solution? Change habits and attitudes, starting with yourself. Don't mimic others. Try to be number one in hospitality and sportsmanship.

*Practice the habit of doing unto others.*
How? JUST DO IT!

# Too Much Time at the Complaint Counter

Do you realize that scads of people spend much of their life at the complaint counter? If you doubt it, ask someone who serves the public or is a manager of a business. Stack or add up your thanks against complaints for the last week. Complaints came out on top, right?

If you want a pleasant surprise, try this. The next time you are in a shop or business and have been served well, ask to speak with a manager and share something positive about the store or service. Don't be shocked when you first see the manager with an anxious look on his face. As you express a compliment, the worried look will transform into a grateful smile and the manager will not be able to thank you enough. Do you know why? Ask him and he will tell you "we are engulfed with complaints, but few words of thanks."

Recently I had a pleasant stay in a Seattle hotel. Before leaving, I left a note complimenting the staff and the hotel. Believe it or not, I received letters from two executives thanking me for my comments. I could hardly believe one, let alone two! It's a pleasant surprise.

TWO PLEASURABLE HABITS TO PRACTICE:

    1. Make a habit of sharing compliments
    2. Stay at the compliment counter

*If you practice these habits,*
*you will think you have died and done gone to heaven.*
*So will your friends.*

# The Main Thing is the Main Thing

"The main thing is the main thing." This is an unusual expression frequently used by some people.

For many, the main thing is their own thing, and so they do exactly what they want — they lie, cheat, steal, hate, lust, criticize and follow their own repulsive appetites. This appears to be the attitude and belief of those who develop their own value system. They forget responsibility and plain ol' common sense and courtesy to others. This is like the man who was asked, "How many Ps are there in the word apologize?" The man said, "I don't know, I never use the word."

I read about a man who said he had gotten divorced because he felt he was entitled to some happiness. He was really saying that he didn't care about anyone else. I've had friends tell me: "No one, not even my doctor, is going to tell me what to do." Nobody did and can now, because these friends have already departed to meet their maker.

The main thing for many husbands, wives and teens is that they want to have their freedom. So they get divorces, slam-dunking their spouses and children in the process. People who want to live free, and do only as they please, often become emotional cripples and slaves to the habits which eventually kill them. The major decision for their loved ones is what kind of casket to purchase.

If you doubt the enormity of sorrow created by those who live by the main-thing attitude, ask those trampled over by the main-thingers, who believe they have the right to ignore their actions and their responsibilities to family and community. This thinking is best expressed in the Grammy-winning song "All I Wanna Do" is have some fun before I die.

When everything is said and done, my Uncle Joe expressed it best: "When the final count is in, and you have cashed in your chips, you had better be ready to meet your maker, 'cause they don't sell round trip tickets or give out rainchecks."

If you swallow the idea of the main thing, your thinking process is irrational. I would suspect you are missing a few bricks on the top floor. My suggestion is that you read Uncle Joe's advice about five times and do some serious soul-searching.

# Don't Be Paralyzed By Fear

Seems like the whole world is paralyzed by fear.  Many are so stressed out that they can't enjoy a normal life.  For some it's like being in a pitch-dark tunnel without an exit.  Fear can be frightening.  I am not saying there is an easy solution, but we must learn to control our fears or our fears will conquer and control us.

I read the story of a man who complained because the crowing of his neighbor's rooster kept him awake at night."  The neighbor said, "I don't understand it. The rooster only crows two or three times a night."  The man replied, "That's not the problem. It's waiting for the rooster to crow that keeps me awake."  Many of us are like that man, if we don't have something to fear, we magnify imaginary and needless fears.  There are times you will think that fear has beaten you up, knocked you down, and stomped on you.  We do have to deal with real fears, but we don't have to focus on them.

The writer of Psalm 34:4 knew where to turn when his mind was distressed and fearful.  He said, "I cried to the Lord and he answered me!  He freed me from all my fears."  When confronted by fear, repeat this verse to yourself.  It can relieve your mind of stress and give you peace of heart.  This is the peace Jesus promised in John 14:27.

The struggle with fear is a seemingly never ending battle.  If we recognize fear for what it is, cease depending upon self-made solutions, and trust our fears to God, we will discover He is our refuge and a tested help in time of trouble.  Here is a little secret that will bless you and others.  Find someone who is discouraged and defeated by fears.  Share with them the promises of Psalm 34:4.  Let them know what God has done for you and what He can do for them.

# Happiness is a Choice

Did you ever wonder why some people are happy and some miserable, some sad and some glad, some have a smile and others have a frown?  Believe it or not, happiness is a choice. A dear Quaker lady was asked to explain her obviously youthful appearance, her appealing vivacity and winning manner.  She replied sweetly, "I use for the lips—TRUTH, for the voice—PRAYERS, for the eyes—PITY, for the hands—CHARITY, for the figure—UPRIGHTNESS, for the heart—LOVE."  How's that for a facial makeup kit?

A friend told me that bitterness, anger, and hate all leave their mark on our face in the form of wrinkles.  Bitterness is especially easy to see on a person's face.  Remember, it takes fewer muscles to smile!  There is not one of us that doesn't look better with a smile.

A large billboard on a major street in Tampa, Florida read, "HATE and RAGE are four letter words, but so are LOVE and HOPE.  Hey, you got a choice."  You can choose hate, envy, lust, bitterness, jealousy, selfishness, and complaining OR you can choose love, joy, peace, patience, kindness, goodness, gentleness and self-control.  One fact is certain, if you make the right choices, your family and friends will be happier and maybe your dog won't bark and howl so much.  Trust me, you'll look better with a smile!

# CS and GW

Susie told me, "You could surmise, I'm not genius. I don't have a Ph.D. or even a super IQ.  But I did have something going for me. It was CS and GW.  My mother gave me CS and GW which literally made me what I am today.  You see, my father died when I was eight years old.  I had three brothers and one sister.  I became the papa, mama, sister, and brother because Mama had to work to keep clothes on us and food in our mouths. Every day, to us kids, she was the mother of the year.

"Mama's CS and GW helped me to have a happy home, a fine husband and three super kids.  When I was a teenager I had some so-called friends who kept telling me to come and run with the crowd.  They said they had fun, fun, fun. Lots of easy money, drinks on them, and sleep with whoever, whenever.  They told me not to miss it because it was a great time.  I chose not to join them because I remembered Mamaís CS and GW.

"I hope you understand it is marvelous and terrific to have a Ph.D. and an exceptional IQ. But it's even better to possess CS and GW.  I'll tell you why.  Today, I have a fine family and a happy home because my mom told how to possess and use COMMON SENSE (CS) and GODLY WISDOM (GW).  And I had enough sense to listen to my mom."

# You Don't Want to be Lucky!

Have you ever said "Man, I sure was lucky today?" Would it upset you if I said the word lucky should never be in your vocabulary? Now the world will not come to an end if you use the word, but it is best not to. I read about a cowboy who applied for insurance and the agent asked him if he had ever had any accidents. The cowboy said "No, but I was laid up some time ago when I was bit by a rattlesnake and kicked by a horse." The agent responded, "I thought you said you never had any accidents?" The cowboy responded, "I haven't. The snake and the horse bit and kicked me on purpose - it wasn't an accident."

Life can bite, kick and be harsh - and it will not be by accident, it will be on purpose. The synonyms for luck are chance or accident. We're in trouble if our life is based on luck instead of faith. If we attempt to succeed by luck alone, it will be a one-way street to dismal failure. We may have short periods of unpredictable success, but it will endure about as long as the man who built his house on sand instead of rock. Facts of life assure us that bonafide happiness results from faith and from diligent, conscientious effort.

I would suggest we remove the word luck from our stock of words and thank God that faith is available. As Kousin Zeke said, "We shore would be blessed if we decided who we is, why we is here, and where we is headed."

# Focus on NOW

I have friends who never enjoy life.  Do you know why?  They live in yesterday.  They are like the multitudes who never delight in anything that depicts happiness.  Their focus is on the past.  As Uncle Joe said, "They dwell on the mournful, dismal, sick, dying and dead."  Even when life is on a halfway even keel, they worry because they haven't got anything to worry about.  For them, there is no light at the end of the tunnel and the glass is always half empty.

A man said to me, "I always try to live one day at a time."  I reminded him, "That's not bad, but actually we can only live one second at a time."  Guess what?  That second has already passed!  But thank God more seconds are on the way for our use to bless and help others.  Never forget, the past is over, done, gone, finished and terminated.  If that is true, what in this cotton pickin' world is a person to do?  Really it's not that complicated or difficult to understand.  You just:

1. Forget the past and move on.
2. Learn from our goof-ups, sins, and mistakes.
3. Know that yesterday is dead and gone - tomorrow is yet to come.
4. Thank God you have this MOMENT, NOW, to make things smack-dab right.
5. Be available to make this a happier and better world.
6. Remember that regardless of how bad you think you have it, someone else has it much worse.
7. Remember that IT ONLY TAKES ONE PERSON TO MAKE A DIFFERENCE IN THIS WORLD....

**YOU BE THAT PERSON!**

# Listen Up

I read about a man who said, "After 12 years of therapy, my psychiatrist said something that brought tears to my eyes. He said 'No Hablo Ingles'." It's a joke, but sad to say there is more truth than fiction to it. Most of us are poor listeners and communicators. One reason is because we are too full of our own opinions and ideas and hardly listen to what others try to tell us. Often we cannot give others a simple answer or response. Why? Because we are too busy trying to scheme and figure out how to get our point across - right or wrong (usually more wrong than right). This occurs with children, youth, husbands, wives, in-laws, out-laws, friends, and neighbors.

This is illustrated by a judge interviewing a woman regarding her pending divorce.

> *"What are the grounds for your divorce?"*
> *"About four acres with a nice little brick house."*
>
> *"No, I mean what are your relations like?"*
> *"They are fine. I have an aunt living here in town, as do my husband's parents."*
>
> *"Does your husband ever beat you up?"*
> *"Yes, about twice a week he gets up earlier than I do."*
>
> *"Why do you want a divorce?"*
> *"Oh, I don't want a divorce. I've never wanted a divorce. My husband does. He says he can't seem to communicate with me."*

This sounds foolish, but for many of us it hits home even though we will not admit it. I've got a thought. Wouldn't it be great if we shifted our tongues out of gear, shut our mouths and opened our ears; then prayed for a little Godly Wisdom and Common Sense — then began to use it. As the farmer said, "It shore would make your friends, and even your enemies, happier and keep you out of a heap of trouble."

# The Greatest Thing

Everyone wants a sure-enough, bonafide, true friend because true friends are difficult to scare up.  Kousin Zeke says,  "Forget about finding the perfect friend.  He probably wouldn't like you anyway."  Socrates once asked a simple man what he was most thankful for.  The man replied, "That being such as I am, I have the friends I have."  Understand, a true friend accepts us as we are, loves unconditionally as Jesus taught, encourages, lifts us up and is always loyal.  The author of this poem says it best:

<u>The Greatest Thing You Will Ever Make</u>

*Oh, you can make a lot of money,*
*Make a cake sweet as honey*
*Make a photograph that's wonderful to see,*
*But no matter how long it takes,*
**THE GREATEST THING YOU WILL MAKE IS A FRIEND**

You want to be happier and make others happier?  Get into the friend making business.  Kousin Zeke says, "Some folks ain't got no friends 'cause they don't make no friends."

*It shore would be a heap of help*
*if we started making friends* TODAY. NOW.

# What Bugs You?

What bugs you? What is your number one worry? Fear and worry come in the same basket. Worry can steal your energy and happiness. I have friends who have absolutely no cause to worry, but they manufacture reasons. They can find a fear or dread under every rock. Someone wrote, "There are two things to worry about: Are you well or sick? If you are sick, there are two things to worry about: Will you get well or die? If you get well, there is nothing to worry about. If you're going to die you'll be so busy checking on your friends, you won't have time to worry." Don't believe this for one instant.

Kousin Zeke sez, "I read in the Good Book, "What does it benefit a man if he gains the whole world and loses his soul in the process? Is anything worth more than the soul? I don't know 'bout you, but it appears it would help to have a soul check to learn if they is going up or down. Before you shut your eyes tonight, say something like this: "Lord, forgive me. Help me to know where my soul is gonna go when I cash in my chips. Don't just wish it, say it... "Lord, Help Me." If you mean business, he will, because he's in the soul and happiness business."

# Be a Lighthouse

I read about a ship's captain, on a foggy night, who saw what appeared to be the lights of another ship heading toward him.  He instructed the signalman to contact the other ship by signal light.  He sent this message: "Change your course 10 degrees to the North."  The reply came, "Change your course 10 degrees to the South."  The Captain responded "I'm a Captain, change your course."  Response, "I'm a seaman first class, change your course."  The Captain was furious and responded, "I'm a battleship, you change your course 10 degrees to the North."  Reply, "I'm a Lighthouse - you change your course."  I can assure you that the Captain changed his course.

Would you rather be in charge of the lighthouse or be the captain of the battleship?  I know people the world would classify as persons of success, fame, and status.  I mean they have reached the top rung - they are Captains.  If you doubt it, ask them.  These Captains are so enamored with themselves, they have no concern for others.  Being Captain is a major problem in the world, workplace, home, politics, Little League and big league.  The problem is that Captains always want to bat. If they can't, they take their bat and go home. Jesus often dealt with Captains and he had to remind them that he came to serve, not to be served.

If you are searching for a life of peace and joy, become involved with a lighthouse that is a light for the lonely, needy and less fortunate.  Begin to share TLC - Tender Loving Care.

*If you are tempted to act like a Captain,* JUMP SHIP!

# Keep On Keepin' On

A man was driving a worn out car on a desolate road when the engine died.  As he coasted to the side of the road, another car drove up and stopped. The driver got out and asked, "What's wrong?"  The troubled man replied, "I wish I knew."  The stranger opened the hood, tinkered with something, then signaled the driver to turn the ignition key.  When the car started, the amazed driver shouted, "Thanks. I was afraid the engine had failed for the last time."  The rescuer replied, "Every car has at least one more start in it, if you can get a spark."

This is a comforting lesson.  If you feel like you have gone down for the third time or lost all hope, don't give up.  Have a little faith.  As long as one spark of hope remains, it is never too late to begin anew.  Never surrender or yield a white flag. Just keep on keepin' on.

# Are You Worth Two Cents?

A bumper sticker on an old dilapidated sports car read. "This is it - that's it." Did you ever wonder if you were worth two cents? Or if you had ever accomplished one thing that is worth two cents? Most do their duty, get paid, clip the grass, never miss their pet hobby, watch TV, and TV, and more TV. Then they wonder, isn't there more to life than this? A poem in *Apples of Gold* tells how to obtain a meaningful and fruitful life:

> *Do all the good you can*
> *By all the means you can*
> *In all the ways you can*
> *In all the places you can*
> *At all the times you can*
> *To all the people you can*
> *As long as ever you can*

The poem is not saying get all you can, but to give and be all you can. Not just make a living, but make a life — then share that life. It's funny, but true, you will be happier. And guess what? You will be worth more than two cents. Now ain't that a happy thought?

# Road Maps

What is your opinion of someone who begins a long trip without inquiring about directions or asking for a road map? Stupid? Ignorant? Careless? Today, life's roads are cluttered with people living in turmoil and confusion with no sense of direction - sort of like a man riding a run-away horse without a bridle.

The good news is that guidance and direction are available. Be thankful for caring friends, families, teachers, counselors, and clergy who will try to guide us safely through the mine fields of life. We just need to ask for help.

If you are on the wrong road, or maybe just a deserted side road, feeling lonely and confused, give a holler and someone will be there to help you find the right and better way.

# Planting Potatoes

I read about a farmer sentenced to jail for 60 days at the beginning of the planting season, yet his entire income depended on his potato crop. His wife sent a note to him in prison saying, How am I going to dig up the field and plant the potatoes all by myself?" Knowing that the jail officials read all inmate mail, the farmer sent an immediate reply, "Whatever you do, don't dig up the field, that's where the money is hidden." A week later his wife wrote back, "Somebody must be reading your mail because some men came by and dug up the field. What do I do now?" "Plant the potatoes," he replied.

We may not need to plant potatoes, but it certainly would help if we used common sense and intellect when making decisions and solving problems. The right decisions can keep us out of the dog house - the jail house, too! Now ain't that a happy thought?

# Don't Turn Off the Alarm!

I read about a family having a birthday party. They took the battery out of the fire alarm so that the birthday candles wouldn't set it off. The party was fabulous, the alarm didn't go off, but the house burned down.

Your conscience is comparable to a fire alarm. It's not there just to bug you. You shouldn't cut it off at every passing whim. Your conscience can teach you right from wrong and how to avoid the high cost of foolishness.

You want to be a happy and responsible person? Listen and obey your conscience. Don't turn it off at every inclination or fantasy. Never forget, IT IS BETTER TO BE SAFE THAN SORRY.

# Forgiven

In a cemetery not far from New York City is a headstone engraved with a single word: FORGIVEN. The message is simple. There is no date, only a name, and one lonely word - FORGIVEN.

Forgiveness is one of the most comforting words in the dictionary if we know we are forgiven, and if we are forgiving. A psychologist at a large state university said, "If all my patients understood the actual meaning of forgiveness, I would lose half of them."

Be thankful if you know you are forgiven. Be thankful if you are not, because you can ask and receive forgiveness.

*Remember, forgiveness is always available*
*- to receive or to give to another.*

# Make Every Day Thanksgiving Day

Today is not Thanksgiving, but have you ever heard the statement, "Every day should be Thanksgiving?" I read about a family traveling to visit their relatives for Thanksgiving. On the way, their car began to give them trouble. After several hours' delay, they finally found the needed parts. They arrived very late the night before Thanksgiving. The next day, some family members caught the flu. It was a miserable Thanksgiving Day. To make matters worse, on the way home the baby became ill. Worn out and discouraged, they continued home in silence. Then one of the smaller children piped up, "Whatever happened to Thanksgiving?" When life erupts, plans fail, and disappointments come,. Stop and take a moment to count your blessings.

It doesn't take a genius to discover that, regardless of your situation, there is always someone "worser off" than you. If we attempt to make every day Thanksgiving Day, then we won't have to ask, "whatever happened to Thanksgiving?"

# God Never Sleeps

Where is your security, hope for the future, finances, health or family? I read about two men. One looked forward to a monthly check at retirement - he is now without a job. The other man, who anticipated a happy retirement, is now terminally ill. According to the story, these two men said, "We do not live in continual worry. We trust God and the advice of someone who told us that the God who cares for us never sleeps. We see no sense in both of us staying awake."

Remember Jesus, the one who offers hope, never, never changes. The happy news is that he is the same yesterday, today, and tomorrow.

# Passing Grades

Does it ever cross your mind just how smart, talented and loving you are? If the need should arise, you will even assist a neighbor, if convenient. On a scale of 1 to 10, you would rate yourself a 9, possibly a 10. But according to one authority, if you possessed the virtues mentioned above, but did not possess love, your grade would be a double zero (00). He said, "Love is patient and kind, never jealous or envious, boastful or proud, never haughty, selfish or rude; does not demand its own way. It is not irritable or touchy. It does not hold grudges and will hardly even notice when others do it wrong, but is never glad about injustice, but rejoices when truth wins out."

By these standards, it would appear very difficult to receive a decent grade. but with honest heart-searching effort, you could chalk up a passing grade. For certain, you, your family, and your friends would be much happier. A word of caution: some of your friends may faint.

# A Googolplex Christmas

Did you ever hear the word GOOGOLPLEX? The word was coined by Edward Kasner, a mathematician. The number 10 raised to the power Googol; in other words the number 1 followed by 100 zeros. That figure blows my mind. No one can comprehend the magnitude of such numbers. Space and time are GOOGOLPLEX.

Today, most people are searching for just a dab of good news or a little peace of mind happiness. For certain, you cannot obtain good news from the newspapers or TV. If you watch TV news too much you may end up depressed and living on upset street. Believe me this ain't GOOGOLPLEX news.

Let me tell you about some GOOGOLPLEX news. It's not new but it is so wonderful and amazing our minds can hardly comprehend its magnitude. The wonderment is that this news was announced by the angel, Gabriel, in Luke 2:10,11, to some shepherds in a field guarding their flock of sheep.

The shepherds were badly frightened, but the angel reassured them: "DON'T BE AFRAID!" he said. "I BRING YOU THE MOST JOYFUL NEWS EVER ANNOUNCED, AND IT IS FOR EVERYONE! THE SAVIOR - THE MESSIAH - HAS BEEN BORN TONIGHT IN BETHLEHEM!" This is what I call GOOGOLPLEX news. It's for everyone or anyone: the lonely, depressed, fearful, up-and-outers, down-and-outers and whosoevers. The icing on the cake: it's free. Allow no circumstances to prevent you from receiving the true message of a GOOGOLPLEX CHRISTMAS. Then share the GOOGOLPLEX NEWS with others.

# A Sad or Glad New Year

Kousin Zeke sez, "If the creek don't rise and the chickens don't fly away, you and me will have a SAD, BAD, or GLAD New Year." Believe it or not, we have to vote. It's a vote to be HAPPY or UNHAPPY. I've already voted. What about you? You say, "Jack you gotta be missing some bricks on the top floor. You don't understand my sorrowful situation. I live a daily life of dread, not joy. Happiness ain't for me."

I can't give you a happy pill but Jesus can give you something better. Once he was talking to some DO-GOODERS who only did good for themselves. Their motto was EAT, DRINK and be MERRY. Do what feels good. He gave them and us a set of basic values for happiness:

*Happy are those who are humble and gentle*
*Happy are those who depend on God*
*Happy are those who are just and good*
*Happy are those who are kind and merciful*
*Happy are those who have pure hearts*
*Happy are those who strive for peace*

John Walvoord said, "These values only produce joy when we are properly related to God through faith and place our complete trust in Him." The average Joe and Jane won't buy this set of values, that's why they are so miserably unhappy. If you desire contentment and happiness in the New Year, LIVE BY THESE VALUES. Kousin Zeke sez, "He do."

# Excuses Won't Work

Did you hear about Tom, Dick, and Harry? A friend had a desperate need and asked them for some immediate assistance. Tom said, "I"m much too busy." Dick said, "I've been sick." Harry replied, "I want to, but I'm working on my house." This is not just a current news story. Jesus had a similar problem with some of his so-called followers. He told the story of a man who prepared a feast and sent out invitations. One of the invited guests said, "I just bought some land." Another said "I just bought five pair of oxen." One replied, "I just got married and you know I can't."

Kousin Zeke sez, "They tells me the road to Hell is paved with good intentions. I don't know if them is good intentions or excuses. One fact I know, I ain't been born on no turnip wagon and it don't take no genius to figger out, when we miss an opportunity to help others, we miss a ton of happiness."

GUESS WHAT? The time may come when you are more than desperate for some help. You will thank God for folks who do not use EXCUSES. Fact is, they don't have the word EXCUSE in their vocabulary. ANOTHER GUESS WHAT. YOU WILL BE HAPPILY SURPRISED AT THE BLESSINGS YOU CAN GIVE AND WILL RECEIVE. You'll even sleep better.

# The "Know I Can Train"

Do you remember the story of the LITTLE TRAIN that had difficulty climbing a hill? It puffed and puffed and kept repeating, "I think I can" until the little CHOO CHOO realized it could. Then it repeated, "I know I can" and it did.

Lots of folks think like the LITTLE CHOO CHOO TRAIN. They've been reared with the attitude, "I think I can't" and believe it or not they can't. They could, if effort were used with a little faith and a big dose of I KNOW I CAN.

I don't know the author of this one verse poem, but it sums up the story of the LITTLE CHOO CHOO TRAIN:

> I'm only one
> But I'm one
> I can't do everything
> But I can do something
> And what I can do
> I ought to do
> And what I ought to do
> By the grace of God
> I can and will do

If we can take to heart this poem, there is no situation, problem or mountain that we cannot conquer.

# Bury Pride

Joe said to Leroy, "Leroy, you don't pay your bills. What your friends gonna say when you die?" Leroy said, "The same thing they said about Uncle Peter when he died."
"What's that?"
"Bury him."

Is there more to life than this? Believe me there is. What's your opinion of a murderer, a thief, a liar or someone who is deceitful and slanderous? It's easy to hate these types of persons and if possible condemn them to Hades. Their habits should be condemned. Jesus gave a catalog of all the above sins BUT HE ALSO INCLUDED PRIDE. Do you know the meaning of PRIDE? It is BOASTFULLY EXALTING ONESELF ABOVE OTHERS with moral and spiritual insensitivity; in plain ol' English, it's PREJUDICE. Are you guilty?

Kousin Zeke sez, "For most of us, it's our thinking, thought-life that pollutes our minds and makes us unfit. This ain't nothing to sneeze at, 'cause one of these days you and me is gonna stand before our MAKER and I don't want to hear, Kousin Zeke depart from me, I don't know you." Let's each of us remember that life is more than what they said about Uncle Peter, BURY HIM. If PRIDE IS A MAJOR PART OF OUR THINKING, let's ask for FORGIVENESS, change our THINKING and ATTITUDE, then BURY PRIDE and PREJUDICE FOREVER. Guess what? You and your dog will be HAPPIER AND SO WILL THIS WORLD.

# Gripes and Grumbles

Some questions we should ask ourselves: Are we like GRUMPY, one of the seven dwarfs? Do we GRIPE, GRUMBLE AND COMPLAIN constantly? Better yet, do I want to know what a GROUCH I am? Did you ever hear this statement: "It's better to be corrected in the school room than to have the world laugh at you." In other words, it's better for someone to be up front with us, tell us the truth, than for the world to laugh at us. One way to find out, if you're not chicken-hearted, ask a close friend or family member if you're on speaking terms.

Kousin Zeke sez, "This ain't no PHILOSOPHIZING but most of us ain't much for hearing the truth, especially 'bout ourselves. We loves laudable praises and bouquets most." King Solomon, one of the wisest men, hit the nail on the head. He said, "THE ADVICE OF A WISE MAN REFRESHES LIKE WATER FROM A MOUNTAIN SPRING. MY WORDS ARE PLAIN AND CLEAR TO ANYONE WITH HALF A MIND, IF IT IS ONLY OPEN." Kousin Zeke sez, "If I wuz you I'd stop listening to the one who looks back in the mirror." Together let's take heed to the advice of Solomon, be certain our minds are open, get rid of all the GRIPES and GRUMBLES and replace them with PRAISES and THANKS. FOR CERTAIN, you will FEEL BETTER, LOOK BETTER and even have MORE and BETTER FRIENDS. Can't beat this with a stick.

# One Second at a Time

From this SECOND until the same SECOND one year from now, you and I will have 36,536,000 SECONDS to use or misuse. How many SECONDS do you have left on this earth? Many believe they have three score and more years, while planning for a life of success and ease. At least they seem to spend most of their waking hours seeking those things. The younger generation thinks, plans and lives like tomorrows are forever.

I hate to BUST YOUR BUBBLE but everyone has only one SECOND at a time. Hey, a SECOND just passed me by. It's gone forever. But thank God here comes another one that I can use or misuse. Jesus, The Master Time Keeper, had some followers who spent all their SECONDS trying to get MORE and more goodies. This bugged him and he put a sermon on them and us. "Don't store up Goodies here on earth. They can be stolen. Better yet, put your TIME and TALENTS to good use. Don't worry about tomorrow. God will take care of your tomorrow, too."

Kousin Zeke sez, "Don't 'tempt to figger out God's time table fer your last SECOND ON THIS EARTH. Do all the GOOD, spread all the JOY you can. Live for the moment. Don't even waste a single SECOND. Love life, enjoy life. Make every day a series of HAPPY MOMENTS FOR YOU AND OTHERS."

A *good motto*:
**"LIVE ONE HAPPY SECOND AT A TIME."**

# It's Nice to Be Nice

Recently I was in the Atlanta airport and took a shuttle van to the hotel. Before the shuttle driver began he put up a sign for all the riders to read. I pondered what did he want to tell the riders. The sign read:

"It's nice to be important
but it's more important
to be nice."

How does that thought grab you? it grabbed me. I complimented the driver for the sign. He said, "At first the management objected but now it's OK. That's a typical corporate attitude. Somewhere along the line we've lost our COMMON SENSE DECENCY COMPASS." The driver did not possess an academic Ph.D but he did have a very special Ph.D: PERSONAL HAPPINESS DEGREE. He told me, "I'm a Christian and try to be kind and considerate of others." By the way, that's the dictionary's definition of nice: "NICE IS BEING KIND, CONSIDERATE, WELL MANNERED; A MORALLY UPRIGHT PERSON."

It's later than we think. In this mixed-up world life can be like a ROLLER COASTER, SOMETIMES WE'RE UP AND SOMETIMES DOWN. OFTEN WE'RE UPSIDE DOWN. For many it's 100% super to be important. For those who have learned the secret to happiness it's 1000% super to be NICE. READ and MEMORIZE THE SIGN. PRACTICE BEING NICE. Kousin Zeke sez, "There ain't no NICE PILL to make you NICE. But you can JUST DO IT."

# Paddle Fast

A bumper sticker read, "LIFE IS SHORT. PADDLE FAST." Would you like to have a championship team, family, business or career? Most of us would. How, then? A lady basketball player, Michele Marcinick, playing for the University of Tennessee, was told by her coach: "It does not matter whether you score or not. Just get the ball to the other players." To me it sounds like she was told, "You ain't gonna be no star." She did her job. The team won a national championship and she was voted the game's most valuable player. Why? Her coach, Pat Summit, understands a secret for winning. What is the secret? Read on.

Before a SUPER BOWL game a reporter asked the coach of the Green Bay Packers, "Will your quarterback be effective?" The coach replied, "Our winning does not depend on one player. It depends on how well the team performs together." Did it work? yeah. They won the Super Bowl. Think through what Kousin Zeke sez. "It's true, LIFE IS SHORT and WE BETTER PADDLE FAST. If the storms of life is swamping "YO" lifeboat maybe you need another paddler. I did. I climbed into the Lord's boat and I ain't worried 'bout drowning since."

One of the secrets of winning and being victorious in daily life is TEAMWORK. If you are paddling with one paddle, get another one; maybe two. It doesn't require a ROCKET SCIENTIST TO FIGGER OUT THAT WITH ONE PADDLE YOUR BOAT GOES IN CIRCLES. WITH TWO IT GOES STRAIGHT.

*If life is an endless circle, do as Kousin Zeke did.*
*Climb into the Lord's boat.*

# The Bucket

What are you carrying in your bucket? You say, "I don't have a bucket." But you <u>do</u>. A church newsletter stated, "If you were walking and carrying a bucket of water and someone jostled you, there could be spilled from the bucket only that which it contained."

As you walk along the paths of life, people are constantly bumping into you. If your heart-bucket is full of criticism, a nasty temper and a repulsive disposition, only those things will spill from it. On the other hand, if it is full of joy, you will spill smiles and pleasant remarks. Make it a point to fill your bucket to its brim with the better and best things of life. When you are jostled, only the better and best will spill.

I assure you, there is someone with a desperate need for a splash of kindness, and a word of encouragement from you.

# Epilogue

These "Happy Thoughts" were written for the thousands who have turned to God, but who still carry their burdens day after day. Your major obstacle for overcoming worry and not finding peace of mind that you seek may be that you have never personally committed your life to Christ. If you are a Christian, then breathe a prayer of thanks. If you are not a Christian, ask God now in your own words to forgive your sins and come into your heart. Let Him help you trust His judgment instead of relying on your own decisions.

# Don't Underestimate Your Worth

Does it ever cross your mind? I'm not really too good at anything and I guess you could call me a no-talent person. I honestly try, but just can't cut it!

Every Christmas season you and I are blessed by the words and music of *White Christmas*. The movie *White Christmas* has become a TV Christmas tradition. On special patriotic occasions, worship services, events, and holidays, we are inspired by *God Bless America*. At Easter, we are filled with joy and our hearts are lifted up with happiness as we listen to the melody of *Easter Parade*. We are reminded of the true meaning of Easter.

These songs are only three of over 1,000 songs written by a man who immigrated from Russia to America as a small boy. He had no education and no musical training. He wrote every song in the key of "F". His name was Irving Berlin and he became the most famous song writer in American history. His songs are played daily over thousands of radio and TV stations. He was so popular that often movie theaters would put his name over the name of the movie on the marquee.

When you begin to ponder what you can't do and how much talent you don't have, think about Irving Berlin. REMEMBER: with a truck load of SINCERE EFFORT and a DAB OF GOD-GIVEN FAITH you can do anything you set your mind to.

Kousin Zeke sez:
*"You can be somebody 'cause God don't make nobodies!"*

Mary,
So glad that you are feeling better. I thought about you when I read this. You always do more than you think.

Love,
Doris

# Record Your Own Happy Thoughts...

_____

_____

_____

_____

_____

_____

_____

_____

_____

_____

_____

_____